Crime Prevention

Throwing the Book at Criminals

JOHN CORBETT

ISBN: 978-0-578-02180-5

Crime
Prevention

Throwing the
Book at Criminals

JOHN CORBETT

This book is dedicated to the
belief that crimes are learned
behaviors and criminals are
the professors of crimes.

Table of Contents

Introduction..1
Home Protection Techniques...6
Auto Protection Techniques..14
Self Defense Techniques...23
Protective Measures to Prevent Rape..................................28
Preventing Armed Robbery and Theft to Your Business............32
Protecting Your Family or Yourself.....................................37
While Traveling in Vehicles..37
Protecting Your Family and Yourself While........................39
Traveling on Public Transportation.....................................39
Why Communities Need to Start...40
Neighborhood Watch Associations......................................40
Getting Drugs Out of Your Neighborhood..........................43
Getting Your Police Department Involved...........................48
In Community Policing...48
Confronting Alcoholism in Our Society...............................52
Preventing Spousal Abuse..56
Preventing Child Abuse..59
Reducing the Exposure of Violence to Children...................64
Recognizing the New Threat to American Society:
   "Rage"..68
The Types of People Who Commit Crimes...........................71
Dealing With Youths in Gangs..78
Teaching Your Children to Protect Themselves....................80
From Being Abducted, Molested, and Sexually Abused............80
Harvesting Organs From Live Humans.................................83
Preventing Credit Card Usage Theft....................................85
The Future of Crime Fighting Among Law Enforcement............87
Using Automatic Teller Machines (ATM's) Carefully...............90
Recognizing Scams...91
How to Avoid Being a Victim of a Scam.............................119
Preventing Dishonest Repair Service People From
   Victimizing You in Your Home......................................120
The Criminal Population...122
Gun Control..125
Conclusion..127

Introduction

Unfortunately, we will all at one time be a victim of a crime in today's society. Our neighborhoods, streets and shopping centers have become a haven for criminals who think they have a license to commit crimes. We all have heard the suggestion that law-abiding citizens are going to have to take back the streets from the criminals. Many states have already passed laws that enable everyday citizens to carry guns. If criminals knew that their lives are also at great risk during the act of a crime, maybe they will start to think twice about committing crimes. There are many things that we can do in our homes and in our communities to protect ourselves that we may never have thought about doing. Fear has paralyzed us to the point that we cannot think to prevent some things that may not otherwise would have occurred if we had just given some serious thought to the situation.

Many people think that you have to spend a lot of money on expensive security systems or live in upscale neighborhoods to prevent crimes. Obviously being able to afford to do these things will reduce the risk of crime. But we all cannot afford to do this to avoid the risk. The best prevention to crime is common sense which we all should use but sometimes do not think about.

Crime prevention is a number one priority in today's society. If you ask any police officer in your city they will tell you the same thing. We have to start thinking seriously about preventing crime as we do about preventing diseases that affect our well-being. We should think about crime in the same manner. The criminals are certainly planning their next victim and waging criminal warfare against our neighborhoods. It would be remiss for us to simply do nothing and wait for ourselves to be victimized.

I have prepared these crime prevention techniques to help people fight crime. I will certainly try not to frighten you but help you to think about things that may help you to protect yourself. I have learned many safeguards from other sources that I will share with you to learn how to prevent crimes.

Remember that we are in a war against crime and law-abiding citizens are doing whatever they can do to win. When you are in any war you have to be better prepared than the enemy.

When we speak of security, we must think in terms of keeping ourselves safe and secure as possible. The criminal's days are numbered. We all should take an active stand against crime and not wait to react to a situation.

The "Need to Know" method is used by various intelligence agencies in the federal government. This is a classification attached to government agencies that need a security clearance designed to need to know certain classified information from other agencies in order to successfully complete their mission. The "Need to Know" method works because we all should tell people only information that we think they should know about us. The less people know about your home and property is one of the best ways to secure yourself. It is very unfortunate that many home burglaries are committed because the burglar knows or has some association with the victim. Many times it is a relative or friend in disguise who breaks into your home or car. Many burglars case your neighborhood and learn from other people what you have in your home or car.

More than five million people will be victimized by crime in the coming year according to U.S. Bureau of Justice statistics reports. The majority of the crimes will be committed by crack addiction and other drugs that people rob and steal for. Crime is tearing through every fabric of American society.

The myth that inner city youths are responsible for the vast amount of crimes is getting farther and farther from the truth. It is true that many crimes are committed by inner city youths. But all types of people are committing crimes regardless of where they live. The reason that crime is high is directly related to unemployment, drugs and poverty. Drugs are not just concentrated in the inner city, they are everywhere. Many factories are shutting down in cities and drug dealers are headed to those cities to set up shops. Even small town factories are closing and putting people out of work. A small town in Texas in 1995 saw its crime rate triple as a result to a high rise to crack addition. Most people have the notion that crimes are committed by indecent and criminally-prone people. If this is all true, how do you explain the rise in crimes being committed by people in upper-class neighborhoods? Crime is almost inescapable and

Americans will have to do whatever it takes to prevent the

likelihood of being the next victim. Americans will have to

lobby to politicians for more jobs, more money for education and

an increase in moral values in the country.

Home Protection Techniques

The first thing anyone would say when you mention that you want to protect your home from being burglarized is to suggest that you buy a home security system. But what do you do when you cannot afford to buy one? Security systems are very popular and there are many different models and prices on the market. But if you cannot afford one, there are other measures you can take to help secure your home.

Listed below are many things you can do to help protect your home:

1. Cut down any small trees, large bushes and shrubs that block the view of the entrance or windows to your home.

2. Never leave a note on a door telling anyone you are not at home.

3. Never leave any doors unlocked.

4. When you purchase a garage door opener, change your code on your opener as soon as it is installed.

5. All windows should be locked at all times. However, never use window locks that you need a key to open. Never nail your windows shut preventing opening them in case of a fire.

6. Never leave any ladders outside your home.

7. Never advertise that you are going away on a trip or vacation for service people.

8. Never leave keys under mats or hide them in obvious places.

9. Do not put your name and address on identification key chains.

10. Always keep your house keys and your car keys separate.

11. Use plenty of lights around your house. Motion sensitive lights are the best kind.

12. Leave lights on if you expect to enter your home after dark.

13. Always beware of strange vehicles around your home.

14. Never leave large amounts of cash in your home.

15. Hide very expensive items such as jewelry in inconspicuous places.

16. All exterior doors should have double entry deadbolt locks. Double entry deadbolts require a key to be used on both sides of the door. The deadbolt should be one full inch long to increase its effectiveness. The keys should be stored in the home where everyone knows where they are with easy access.

17. Install a peephole on doors that are solid and do not have any glass to see through.

18. On sliding glass doors, place a steel rod in the bottom inside track so that it cannot be easily pushed back. Sliding doors should have screws installed in the underside of the overhead track to prevent them from being removed out of the track. The screws should be installed about one foot apart and backed out about one half inch so that the doors cannot be lifted out of the track. Most sliding glass doors do not come with a keyed lock. If your doors do not have these, install them. There are many types on the market that you

can purchase, one type is a lock which fastens to the outside door and when locked with a key the pin cannot be removed.

19. Steel security bars made of ornamental iron can be used to cover windows with large areas of glass. If you purchase these security bars, make sure they have an easy way to be pushed out to open in case of a fire. If they have locks on them and the key is to the inside simply leave the key in the lock at all times. You can do the same for your deadbolts when you are at home.

20. Your property should be engraved in your home with an engraving machine. Anything that is portable should be engraved with a personal ID number such as your driver's license or your social security number. Be careful to not engrave on areas of your property that may devalue it.

21. You should photograph your property and keep records of serial numbers in a safe place. Your photographs and serial numbers should be kept by a relative or a friend if you do not have a safety deposit box. They

should not be kept in your home in case of fire or disaster.

Many people buy dogs for protection of homes. Having one in the back yard or in the house is one of the best protections a homeowner could have. If you do not like animals, buy a "Beware of the Dog" sign and place it in your window or on a fence that surrounds your property. This method that I have introduced you to is called the "Need to Know" method. This method is called the "Need to Know" method because no one needs to know what you have at your home other than yourself and your family.

Burglars and intruders have second thoughts about entering a home that may have a surprise waiting for them. If you do not have a burglar alarm at your home, you could buy a sticker that suggests that there is one on the premises. By putting a sticker on each window would help make a burglar rethink a situation. You could even have a sign made to conveniently tell an intruder that poisonous snakes are kept inside your home. Oddly as this may sound, many people have snakes for pets inside their home and some are even poisonous. Who "needs to know?"

Another way to keep burglars from entering your home when you are out of town or on vacation is to leave lights on a timer. The television also may be put on a timer. If you have a video recorder, you could have a tape made with your voice on it talking to someone to ward off intruders. Many people think that these measures are of great cost to your electric bill. But actually it only costs about five to ten cents more a day to leave a television set or a light on when you are away. If you take these measures to protect your home, you should buy surge protectors to cut off electrical appliances in case of a storm.

A homeowner must try to keep his home attractive and repair things whenever possible. Personal grooming of your property is also an effective way to help prevent crimes. Criminals target neighborhoods and homes that are not well kept. If a neighborhood or home is not well-groomed, criminals think you do not care about your property and care less to report a crime that has taken place. Certainly, you won't have control over neighbors, but if you keep your property looking good, your neighbors will start doing the same thing.

When you leave your home for vacations or business trips, you should ask trustworthy neighbors to look after your property when you are gone. Neighbors can help pick up newspapers and take mail from the box. Many people have the newspapers and mail deliveries stopped when they are out of town.

If you live in rural areas where homes are far apart, you should have a light installed near the home on a large utility pole like street lights in the city.

Do not allow service people or solicitors to come in your home without seeing their identification from their business. If you have further doubts of who the person is at your home, call the company office to verify who they are.

I see many homes that have their curtains open day and night so that potential thieves can look into their homes as if they are window shopping. Many people keep their curtains closed 24 hours a day so that people cannot look into their home. If a person has plants that require sunlight during the day, they should at least close them at night.

Going on vacation or long business trips can be enjoyable for you and your family if you have taken precautions to secure your home. Don't discuss your trip in public with anyone. You can notify the police department to patrol your neighborhood and view your home in your absence. Make arrangements for your grass to be cut and your flowers watered. Ask your neighbor to park his extra car in your driveway if you do not have one present.

Organized community watch patrols are very effective in protecting homes. If you do not have one in your neighborhood, I would greatly suggest that you and your neighbors start one. When people see community watch patrols watching neighborhoods, they don't target them.

Your home should be protected as if it is a kingdom because in fact a person's home is his castle.

Auto Protection Techniques

Protecting your vehicle is probably the next thing after your home that you want to have adequately protected. Automobiles cost a great deal of money in these days and many people are keeping them longer than they use to. Losing your car could be very costly to you and may inconvenience you until you can get another one.

Thieves are stealing cars and making enormous profits of the parts. Professional car thieves can break in and steal a car in 40 seconds. Chop shop operators can disassemble parts where they are virtually untraceable. Many cars are repainted and sold to foreign countries.

If you do not have an alarm system on your car, place a sticker on the windows and windshield suggesting that you do have one like you did for your home. People are not going to risk breaking into your car to find out if you do or do not have one. One night my car was parked near a coliseum that was not protected by a security guard. There were about fifty other cars parked there along with mine. The area was well-lighted, but thieves stole the wheels off every other car that did not have a burglar alarm. My car did not have a burglar alarm, but the thieves thought that I did because I had a burglar alarm sticker suggesting that I did. The "Need to Know" method saved my car wheels. My car was not burglarized simply because I had a two dollar sticker on the windshield.

Listed below are do's and don'ts to protect your vehicle:

1. Always lock your car and take the keys with you even if you know you will be gone for about a minute. Unlocked cars account for four out of five car thefts. About one out of five cars stolen have their keys in the ignition.

2. Never leave your car running unattended to warm it up while you go back into your residence. Many cars are stolen out of people's driveways while they are running.

3. Do not hide an extra key on the outside or inside of your car. Many people buy the hide-a-key case that attaches to the bumper and fender to provide

themselves with extra keys. You may not be covered by your insurance if you do something like this.

4.   Roll up windows tightly and securely every time you leave your car. During the very heated summer months you can install sun glare protectors to cool the interior.

5.   Always park in well-lighted areas. Park under street lights or in front of a brightly-lit building.

6.   Always park in locked or security kept garages whenever possible.

7.   Never let anyone test drive your car alone when you are selling it.

8.   Drop a card with your driver's license or your social security number in the window channels and doors. If your car is stolen, this may be one of the only ways to identify your vehicle if it is recovered. One of the first things a thief does is to remove the Vehicle Identification Number commonly called the VIN number.

9. Never leave your license, registration, and the title in your car. Many people have their homes broken into because thieves can trace personal identification inside of your vehicle back to your home. They may use this information to burglarize your home. If your car is paid for and your title is in your car, you may not legally be able to get your car back. Many people give their cars and title to other people. A car thief could very well say that you gave him your car.

Owners of very expensive cars run a greater risk of having their cars stolen. People who have these cars should install anti-theft devices on them.

Here is a list of anti-theft devices that can be used.

1. Steering locks should be installed on the steering wheel such as the popular model called "The Club."

2. Wheel locks which disable the steering of your car. These are steel clamps that should be placed on the wheels.

3. Ignition blocks that kill the engine or block the fuel line.

4.   Car alarms that sounds off in case of unauthorized

     entry.

Park your car very near the location that your are visiting. Never park your car at the mall hundreds of feet away from the entrance. Even though malls have security, they cannot patrol all areas at one time. It is not worth the risk to park far away if you value your car or what's in it.

Car thefts are up in every part of the country. Many people who steal your car are very rarely caught and your car is very rarely found. Car theft has become a billion dollar business for thieves. Experts say that a car is stolen every 30 seconds. The reason car thefts have exploded is because thieves make more money off the parts of cars than selling the cars as one unit. Car manufacturers do not code their parts so that a person can identify their stolen parts to their car. Thieves immediately take your car apart, piece by piece, to sell the parts.

Carjacking can be a very frightening experience by someone who lives through it. If someone approaches you with a gun, don't aggravate them and give them your car. No property is worth risking your life for. To prevent the likelihood that your car will be taken from you, keep your doors locked at all times when you are driving. Be aware of your surroundings and people driving in other cars around you. Another way to prevent carjackings and theft of property is to tint your windows. Real dark windows would be best if the law in your state permits it. What a person can't see inside your vehicle gives them a moment to rethink taking or breaking in your car. It only takes one second to alter the thought pattern of an individual. But if a person is on a drug, they may have a one track mind. Many people are buying a male blow-up "buddy doll" and placing it on the front passenger seat next to them in their cars. A person will not be able to detect that it is a doll when you are traveling on an interstate.

I would avoid putting those very expensive 24 karat gold plated rims on your car. Many thieves and youths in gangs are targeting those wheels because they are gold plated. If you put less expensive custom wheels on your car, buy locks for each bolt. Send for additional keys from the company who manufacture the rims in case you lose one. Locks for each bolt pattern may cost you a little more but it will be worth it in the long run.

If your car is stolen, report the theft to the police and to your insurance company as soon as possible. Don't try to investigate the theft by yourself. Leave it up to the police department to look for your car. It is a good idea to store information in a safe place about your car. The police will want to know in detail the description of your car.

If you can afford and after market car locator, purchase one that tells the police department and car locator's central headquarters where your car is located after it has been stolen.

Listed below is information descriptions to help you provide to the police if your car is stolen.

Year _____

Make _____

Vehicle I.D. Number _____

Model _____

Color _____

Type of Transmission _____

License plate number _____

You should also report any accessories or modifications you have done to your car. Many cars today are customized with styling kits on them. Report any accessories that you have in your car such as stereos, radar detectors and cellular phones.

I like to do research work and case studies before I try to inform anyone on any subject. The case study I did involved using a technique to discourage car theft. I purchased a very inexpensive unique car alarm for my car to use as a deterrent. The alarm looks like an automobile key box used on car lots. It alarms when someone comes up to the car and touches it or otherwise bumps into it. It emits a loud decibel that can be heard for many blocks. When I pass people in my car, I notice people looking inquisitively at the alarms placed on both rear windows wondering what they are.

One day I had to take a neighbor to the bank because she reported some checks that had been taken from her checkbook. She was called to the bank because they caught the offender trying to cash one of the checks. When we arrived at the bank there were about five cars of detectives and a uniform officer there who had arrested the person. When I pulled up in my car, I noticed the police starting to closely observe my vehicle during a bright sunny day. Some of them were standing outside of the bank waiting on my neighbor to come to identify her checks. The police asked in a very concerned way about the alarms and how did they work? I was tickled with pride because I figured that they had probably seen or known of every alarm available for vehicles. I composed myself before I almost started laughing out loud and explained to them what the alarms were.

What that experience taught me was that if you can use anything that will make a person think before they act will be a benefit to you.

Lastly, if you travel a lot, purchase a navigation system for your car to avoid high crime areas. General Motors has an excellent advisory called OnStar. If you cannot afford a navigation system, simply purchase an inexpensive compass to at least tell you what direction you are going.

Self Defense Techniques

A person should always be cautious of being attacked or mugged for any reason with the crime rate as high as it is. Never walk in areas that are not well-lighted and you are alone. If you are walking and you feel that someone is following you, immediately take shelter in a public place.

Women should carry their purses tucked under their arms when they are shopping in stores and returning to their cars. Avoid buying purses with long shoulder straps because they can be easily cut by anyone who wants to snatch it and run. Many women are wearing money belts around their waist to keep someone from taking their money while shopping.

Older persons should carry a walking stick made of a heavy wood to help defend themselves against a potential attacker. You may not need one to support your ability to walk but carry one anyway. Attackers will think twice about someone who is carrying a stick.

There are many self defense classes that are offered such as karate, tae-kwon-do and others that can teach you self defense techniques to help you if you are attacked. But if someone has a weapon, don't challenge them, just give them your property. Your life is worth more than the property. These classes will also help to promote your self-esteem, provide exercise, and give you confidence to go out if you are a single person. If you are attacked and you suspect or know the person is going to rape you, many experts suggest that you do anything such as vomiting or defecating to turn the offender off. Another way is to tell the person you have AIDS, the most dreaded venereal disease. You will probably not have AIDS but your attacker does not need to know that you know. If you suspect the attacker to be insane or on drugs, another way is to try to get him to put on a condom. I would suggest that females carry condoms in their purse. This should be done only at your discretion because if you are raped the police will need strong evidence like the attacker's semen to convict him. Personally I would be more concerned about contracting AIDS. This is a very sensitive subject and whatever you do, try to prevent from being raped. Many people are raped or attacked by a casual acquaintance.

In today's society, there are many single people who live alone. One of the best ways to keep security around your life is not to list your phone number in telephone directories. But if you must do it, request that your address not be listed with your number. If you are out on the town socializing and you meet people who are obnoxious or someone who you feel uncomfortable with, always tell them that you are married with children. Most people don't want to bring people into their lives that will require them to take on more responsibilities. You should always tell people things that will lead them away from you if you do not want to see them again.

Many single people are desperately seeking companions in singles ads, in newspapers and the now new trend, on the computer. This is very risky business when you are dealing with the unknown. I would say that the two best places to meet people are the church and the grocery store. These places are ideal because people are usually being themselves and not putting on airs. Single people think that the best place to meet people is in bars and other places where alcohol is being served. But don't be misguided, these are some of the worst places to meet people who have no character and substance. All people who frequently attend these places are not indecent but very law-abiding citizens. But the vast majority will be there because they are continual losers in the game of life. If you occasionally attend these places, I would strongly recommend not picking up someone there. It is too easy to meet someone there who will take or ruin your life.

I would greatly disapprove of jogging in the late evening alone. It is simply too risky. You should jog in the daylight hours and with a partner if at all possible. People should avoid city parks, national parks and ball fields when they are jogging alone. The best places to jog are in nice residential neighborhoods that have sidewalks.

There are many products on the market that a person can purchase if you do not carry a gun with you. You can purchase chemical sprays, pepper sprays and stun guns from dealers who sell weapons for personal safety. One of my favorites is the pocket size portable alarm that you carry with you. These alarms are carried in your purse or pocket with a string attached to you that sounds off in very high decibel when someone attacks you.

You may have the alarm in your purse and when someone grabs your purse and runs, the alarm will go off in the purse. The attacker will not hold on to the purse with the loud noise and they will immediately drop it.

Protective Measures to Prevent Rape

The taking of a person's dignity such as raping someone is one of the most despicable crimes against a person one can imagine. A woman or a man can be raped at anytime when they least expect it. The best way to protect yourself is to know certain measures taken to prevent rape.

Listed are personal safety tips:

1. Always keep your doors locked at all times when you are at home.

2. List only your house number on your mailbox.

3. Never open your door automatically after hearing a knock. Require the caller to identify himself satisfactorily including repairmen, delivery men and also policemen. Keep your chain bolt attached when checking identification.

4. Leave lights on at night inside and outside your home. Have your key ready to immediately open your door.

5. When a stranger comes to your home and asks to use the phone, make the call for them. Do not let a stranger enter your home.

6. If you notice that a door has been forced open or a window has been broken, do not enter your home. Call the police at a neighbor's house and wait outside your home until they arrive.

7. Keep windows and doors locked on your vehicle at all times.

8. Do not travel frequently on streets that you are not familiar with.

9. Keep your car in gear while you are waiting at traffic lights and stop signs.

10. Check your rear view mirror on your car often while driving. If you believe you are being followed by another car, do not pull into your driveway or park in deserted areas. If the car continues to follow you, drive to the nearest public place and go inside.

11. When parking your car at night, select a place that will be well lit when you return.

12. Never put your name on vanity license plates.

13. After getting off a bus or leaving a subway station at night, look around to see whether you are being followed. If someone is suspicious behind or ahead of you, cross the street several times. If you know a person is following you, don't be afraid to run.

14. If a car approaches you and you are threatened, scream and run in the opposite direction of the car.

15. Walk near the curb and avoid passing close to shrubbery, dark doorways and other places of concealment.

16. If you come home with a friend or by taxi, ask the person to wait until you enter your home.

17. Never get on an elevator with a stranger.

18. Stand near the elevator controls when you enter.

Most of us have heard about people putting a mickey in a drink or food such as Spanish Fly in earlier years. Now there is a new drug on the market that people are using to knock people out to have sex with them. The drug is called Rohypnol and it is being used on unsuspecting victims to rape them. The drug may cause a harmful side effect which creates a symptom like a stroke. People should never accept any food or drink from strangers and especially in a party setting. If someone gives you some food or drink which tastes chalky, you should stop eating or drinking what you have immediately and call for help from the medical profession.

The drug is illegal and brought into this country from Mexico and other countries.

Also, there is another date rape drug called GHP. This drug is in clear liquid form and is undetectable. This drug is usually slipped into drinks of unsuspecting women in bars to be later raped. This drug is very dangerous and has caused some unexpected deaths.

Preventing Armed Robbery and
Theft to Your Business

Convenient stores, fast food stores and small retail operations have become targets for armed robberies because of the easy access to small hand guns in today's society. In the last twenty years, these armed robberies have become so widespread that every city and town is a target regardless of size and population. An armed robbery is a very serious threat to your life and you should take every precaution to prevent one from happening to your business.

Here is a list of prevention techniques you should use to protect your business.

1. Always use at least two people to open and close your business. Leave your business using the front door with one person waiting outside while the other does a final check and lock up.

2. Drive by your business whenever possible when it is closed.

3. Never keep more than twenty dollars in small convenient and fast food stores.

4. A drop safe in the floor should be installed in the floor for large amounts of money.

5. Make frequent bank deposits so that you will not have large amounts of cash on hand. Your bank deposits should be done at various times of the day and not in a routine manner.

6. Never count your money in public view. Use an office with your door locked.

7. Use non-bank bags to conceal that you have money when going to the bank.

8. Keep bait money in your cash drawer serial number of the bills recorded.

9. Keep your business well lighted inside and out.

10. Never install advertising signs that block seeing the entrance to your business.

11. Be aware of suspicious people who hang around your business.

12. Keep the police and emergency phone numbers readily accessible to all personnel.

13. Check employees' employment history and references before hiring them.

14. Install an alarm in your business. The silent types that phone the police department are the best ones.

15. Have employees sign a check sheet for final checking to see if alarms are activated and the premise is secured.

There are certain measures that a person should take during a robbery. Listed are those actions:

1. Do not aggravate the robber. Give the robber exactly what he asks for.

2. Try to be calm and act in slow motions to not panic the robber.

3. Try to give the robber any bait money that you should have in your drawer.

4. Activate your alarm system. You should only activate a silent alarm system. A loud noise may provoke the robber to shoot you.

5. Try to alert some of the other employees. Every business should have some secret hand signals or

words used to tip off other employees to call for help as soon as possible.

6. Try to identify what the robber looks like and what he or she is wearing.

7. Try to identify the weapon that is used in the robbery.

8. Try to look to see what direction the robber went in when he left and what type of vehicle was used.

After the robbery, the victim should:

1. Notify the police as soon as possible to try to have an accurate description for them.

2. Try to remain calm by taking deep breaths.

3. Protect the crime scene as much as possible.

4. Write down your description of the robber and vehicle as soon as possible.

Theft of property is one of the biggest threats to the survival of a business. This crime is usually never solved because of the skill of the people taking your property. You may have taken many of the precautions mentioned in "Protection From Armed Robbery" and that may not be enough to stop a thief. Most of the thefts in the stores occur when there is high traffic or the clerk's attention is distracted.

In 1999, a woman in Utah was convicted of stealing over $250,000 worth of property from businesses in and around Utah. After the woman was convicted and sent to prison for the thefts, she was interviewed on a popular television news magazine show about how she was able to steal from so many stores over and over again. The woman told the television reporter that she was able to pull off the thefts because she was never suspected for theft. The woman was white and never suspected to be a criminal. She was able to take things and stuff them into her personal property by not being in direct view of the video camera. She said she would also take electric tape and cover the electronic codes on the property.

Many black Americans are disproportionately viewed as the only people who will steal from businesses. This ignorance has only given rise to the natural occurrence of the general population to commit and sometimes get away with theft from businesses.

Protecting Your Family or Yourself
While Traveling in Vehicles

Traveling the highways and interstates can be very hazardous to your health if you are not careful. We all like to think of traveling as a joyous experience especially if we are traveling during daylight hours. In today's society, people should never travel alone unless it is an emergency.

Listed are some safety tips to help you while traveling.

1. Always get your vehicle thoroughly serviced before traveling.

2. Phone ahead to the visiting party to let them know that you are coming.

3. Use daylight hours to do most of your driving.

4. Always drive the speed limit.

5. Whenever possible, carry a phone in your vehicle if you are a frequent traveler.

6. Never sleep on the side of the road or in rest areas.

7. Avoid exiting off the interstate in large cities unless you know where you are going.

8. Carry a flashlight with you and high energized batteries.

9. Carry roadside markers and flares.

10. Chart your route on a map before leaving. If you can afford a car navigation system, purchase one to keep you out of high crime areas.

11. Carry an extra gallon of water or antifreeze in the trunk.

12. Carry some tools for minor repairs.

13. Learn how to operate your tire jack before your trip.

14. Wash your vehicle before trips to show that you are not a careless person.

15. Carry enough money, preferably traveler's checks.

16. Keep most of your money in the trunk of your car.

17. If you rent a vehicle, cover up the rental car agent logo with masking or duck tape on the outside of the vehicle.

18. Never pick up hitchhikers.

Protecting Your Family and Yourself While Traveling on Public Transportation

We all have heard of the incidents of crime on public transportation in New York City. Public transportation in large cities is a very risky way to travel with the high incidents of crime on them. Most people use public transportation rather than driving a car because it is much cheaper.

There are some ways to protect your family and yourself on public transportation. Listed are ways to reduce the risk of crime on public transportation.

1. Never show your money while you are riding on public transportation.

2. Never talk to strangers.

3. Never sleep on public transportation unless you are on airplanes or trains.

4. Be knowledgeable of the schedules on public transportation.

5. Keep a close eye on your valuables and your luggage.

6. Always look businesslike when traveling.

Why Communities Need to Start Neighborhood Watch Associations

The police departments help communities to start neighborhood watch associations in most cities. If your police department does not assist citizens in forming these type organizations, you should form your own. The police are not able to patrol all neighborhoods daily because of a lack of manpower. Citizens have to watch out for each other and report incidences of crime when they see them. When criminals know that certain neighborhoods do not have neighborhood watch associations, they become their primary target. Believe it or not, criminals roam neighborhoods to target them.

When a neighborhood watch association was formed in my neighborhood, crime decreased by ninety percent. The mere presence of a sign posted and cars patrolling the neighborhood made the criminals think twice about breaking into homes. Our neighborhood was not crime free; neither was it crime ridden. Regardless of where you live, the chances are good that your home will be burglarized. The only way to greatly reduce the risk is to have manned security to patrol your property at all times.

The most compelling reason that a neighborhood needs citizens to patrol it comes from this experience I had in my neighborhood. On a weekday morning, I observed a car roaming the neighborhood where I live several times. I did not immediately think about what the occupants were looking for. But they were looking for a home to burglarize that morning. I laid down for a morning nap and was awakened by a dog barking. I looked out my window and saw a young man running from my neighbor's home with a pillow case bundled with household items. The burglar ran to a car parked near the home that I had seen earlier. Another person was in the car assisting as the get-a-way driver. I immediately phoned the police and my neighbors to inform them that the home had been burglarized. Because of my observance, the perpetrators were caught trying to sell the items an hour later. If we did not have neighborhood watch, the criminals and the property would have never been found.

The police told my neighbors and me that I was an unusual neighbor because most people say they do not want to get involved. If a neighborhood is to be safe and crime free, neighbors need to watch out for others. I did not see my lookout as being something special, but only concern.

I don't think I would live in a neighborhood that is not concerned about other neighbors. People have to be concerned about others because it is the humane thing to do.

Getting Drugs Out of Your Neighborhood

Illegal drugs are ruining the moral fabric of our neighborhoods and our society in general. Can we afford to just shut ourselves up in our homes and hope it goes away? The drug dealers are hoping we do just that and continue to ignore them. But we cannot afford to ignore this ugly cancer to our society. We have to stop it before it gets any worse. Many innocent people are being hurt and killed as a result of these drugs. Illegal drugs are not just affecting one part of our society as the media would like us to believe. Drugs are entering the well-to-do neighborhoods as well as the poor ones. Too many young children are dying and this is reason enough for us to do something.

Fear has taken control of our lives to the point that we are prisoners in our own homes. It is okay to fear some things because it can be a healthy thing to do. If people didn't have fears, there would be no reason for man to have a supreme being we call God to watch over our lives. We start early to teach our children to fear things that are hot so they will never play with matches. These fears are necessary and part of development which are conditioned fears to protect our children. As our children grow older, we should teach them to not fear things that threaten their livelihood. This means things that keep you from enjoying your life.

Fear should never take over a person's life so that we stop living. It is not easy to beat some fears, but we must never keep from trying. Many things that drug dealers do are cowardly and malicious. We must get rid of them from our neighborhoods. If you have or suspect drug dealers are in your neighborhood, here are some things that we can do to run them out.

1. Take down license numbers of suspected drug dealers in your neighborhood.

2. Take down license numbers of suspected buyers of drugs.

3. Keep a record of what color, type and other description of the cars you suspect dealing in drugs.

4. Keep a record of how often you see these vehicles in your neighborhood.

5. Don't let suspected drug dealers see you record information from their vehicles.

6. Don't tell anyone you do not trust about what you are doing because you could be putting your life in jeopardy.

7. After you have compiled your list, send it to the police department to help in their surveillance.

8. If you wish to remain anonymous for your protection, don't sign your name to any information.

9. Start a citizen group to march in the streets shouting anti-drug slogans in suspected drug dealing areas.

10. Ask the city to tear down abandoned houses and other property that is used in drug use and trafficking.

When you start doing something, you will notice a significant improvement in your neighborhood. I am marveled at a story printed in *Time* magazine, January 1996 issue, about a small town in Texas that was once relatively peaceful began to experience an influx of drugs. Crime got so bad in the town that the residents started a community action group to help them take back their town. The group worked with the police and was instrumental in bringing an expert to help deal with the problem. After some neighborhoods got so bad that you could not sit on your front porch, two sisters, one 79 years old and the other 73 years old, were among the residents affected. The two sisters put their fears aside and joined the local group to help get rid of drugs out of their community. The two sisters stated at the end of the interview that they now can once again sit out on their front porch and enjoy the daylight hours.

Now they could have chosen to stay in their home and do nothing, but they chose to take a stand. Taking a stand against the crime and drugs in their neighborhood was probably the best thing that they could have done for their health. If they could turn around the crime in their town, we can also do things to help reduce crime and drugs in our neighborhood.

The new drug of choice is called "meth" and it has taken over other drugs and their relationship to crime. Every time you hear the news now, it relates to meth labs being busted up and users committing crimes.

The drug has a similar effect as crack cocaine where it produces an immediate sense of euphoria to the user. The user continues to seek this "high" which will never come back as the first sensation.

Meth is produced relatively cheaply and enormous profits are made from the production. People who produce the drug know the risk of the jail time, but they continue to make the drug because of the profits.

Meth destroys the user almost immediately after it has been taken. It will make a person have animal-like behavior and resent anything that is decent in humanity.

The drug will make one's appearance alter and be unrecognizable in only two to three years. They begin to experience tooth decay and loss, dry-like skin, and not be concerned about other personal hygiene.

Meth is a big problem in all parts of the country, but it is appearing to be an epidemic in the Midwest and especially Oklahoma.

Getting Your Police Department Involved In Community Policing

In large cities, community policing is becoming the new effective way to combat crime and keep drugs out of neighborhoods. In fact, community policing is not new and it was practiced in cities many years ago. The police had patrols in cities to walk the streets and keep a friendly rapport with citizens and store shop owners. In today's society and especially in inner cities, the residents need community policing. Many people in these areas feel that the police are not there to serve and protect but to harass and arrest. Everyday citizens will have to work hard and become liaisons between the police and residents. Negative attitudes will have to be changed about policeman in order for them to be effective in communities. We all have heard of the incidents where some bad police have done things to portray negative images of whole police departments. But all police are not bad and many are doing a good job to help keep crime out of our neighborhoods.

People have to start thinking in ways to help their police departments and not alienate themselves from them. In fact, the police need help from the community as well as the community needs the police. When police feel that they are appreciated and needed, they will do a better job for us. When people begin to think in these terms, they will begin to build a bonded relationship between the police and the community. Having a relationship with the community will help reduce the added stress that comes with policing. Many police personnel have been telling us about the enormous stress that goes along with their jobs. Many police do not survive the first two or three years on the force because of the severe stress that is added to the job. Police families are broken up because the stress is taken home to their spouses. Many unfortunate shooting and police physical abuse to citizens may be well contributed to the stress on their jobs.

So we say to ourselves, "What can I do as an ordinary citizen to help my police department?" There are many things that we can do to help our police department other than report crimes after they occur.

Some of the things ordinary citizens can do to help their police departments are:

1. Start a community watch group in your neighborhood if you do not have one.

2. Call the police department's public relations office on non-emergency phone lines to tell them what's going on in your neighborhood, whether it's good or bad.

3. Ask your police department to patrol more in your neighborhoods if you do not have enough patrolling.

4. Ask the police department to establish foot patrols where possible in your neighborhood.

5. Attend city, county, parish, state and other government meetings on policing that are open to the public.

6. Send suggestions to your police departments in the form of letters to suggest other forms of policing in your city or community.

7. Visit your police departments on non-business concerns to be familiar with your police.

8. Start a ride-a-long program in your city with the police to see what it is like on a routine day with a police officer.

You may not be a person with a take charge personality, but somebody has to. The criminals are not going to wait to see if we do not do something to combat crime. They will keep on robbing and stealing from us until we do something.

In my neighborhood we had two street lights that were out for about three years. Many of my neighbors called the proper officials who were responsible for fixing the lights but could not get any action. So I personally started a petition with all my neighbors to get the street lights fixed. When the city officials saw all of those signatures on the petition, we got our street lights fixed the next week. Now this was certainly a non-police matter, but I am only telling this because every citizen has power to get things done. We pay the salaries for the policemen, the police commissioners, and other city officials to serve us as citizens.

Confronting Alcoholism in Our Society

America has never seriously confronted excessive alcohol use as the war we know against illegal drugs. We all are guilty of ignoring abuse of alcohol and especially in our own families until it is too late. We all have heard the saying about alcoholics in families, "It's probably one in your family too." Many families conceal this because it is the great shame of the family. The reason for the ignorance about alcoholism is probably because it is considered a legal drug. Alcohol is a drug and should be treated as a drug in our society. We only hear education about alcohol use until there is a holiday. Education about alcohol use should be all year round and taken seriously. There are countless alcohol-related deaths and rapes of individuals that are directly related to alcohol use. There are many other crimes that are related to alcohol abuse that we all know about.

We should start programs in our schools as we do about drugs to teach our young people early on about the harmful physical and mental effects of alcohol use. Our young people get mixed messages about alcohol use because so many parents

and officials who speak about drugs have serious alcohol

problems. This was one of the strong arguments kids used

against their parents when they were told about the harmful

effects of marijuana and other drugs in the 1960's. Parents who

had alcohol abuse problems would lose their arguments with

their kids every time on ill effects of drug use. The reason

alcohol abuse should be dealt with seriously is because it is so

easy to become alcohol dependent in today's society. Loneliness

is probably the most common contributor to alcohol addiction.

Drinking and driving is the most common problem with

excessive alcohol use. Many police departments constantly

preach this to citizens but we just don't get it. A person who has

a drinking problem should not even own a car if the problem is

out of control. Too many innocent people are killed and hurt by

drunk drivers. One person killed is too many but the statistics

are staggering across the nation. I was certainly glad when the

laws were changed in many states to prosecute drunk drivers as

they are hardened criminals. After many losses of life due to

drinking while driving, many people who are truly sorry that they have taken someone's life. Policemen see this scene too many times and have no sympathy for drunk drivers.

Excessive use of alcohol on college campuses is one of the major contributors to date rapes. It has been widely accepted on college campuses because fraternities and sororities have been using alcohol at their parties and initiations for many years. The old ways will have to be changed because people are becoming alcoholics very early on and hurting themselves and other people. Students in these clubs will have to take a stand against this behavior for changes to come. Building leaders should be the focus of these organizations. Standing against peers who are wrong should be the practice of leaders. Many of these students come from very good homes but never heard strong anti-drinking messages. Because of so many negative incidents involving drinking on college campuses, many officials have abandoned alcohol from college campuses.

The ongoing mission of Mothers Against Drunk Drivers is still effective, but they need help from many other citizens. Their mission is underfunded and they can only advertise effectively during holiday seasons.

If you suspect someone who has an alcohol abuse problem in your home, office or neighborhood, I would try to convince the person to get some help. If the person is unapproachable, you can follow some of the steps that I have listed in the chapter on combating drugs. Alcohol distributors are targeting low-income areas to sell cheap alcohol with very high alcohol contents. Some of the beers and other liquors have much more alcohol contents that the usual cans of beer and liquors that are sold. These high alcohol content beers and liquors are making animals out of people like the crack and other illegal drugs. They are committing crimes against people and property at a very high rate. One of the things that was not included concerning drug sales was picketing the establishment of these businesses. I would start a community action group to run these businesses out of my neighborhood.

Preventing Spousal Abuse

Many women have been trying to get our attention about spouse abuse in our society. Although it is not limited to women who experience spouse abuse in homes, it is more likely that a woman will experience it than a man. Our society treated spouse abuse very lightly until we learned the events surrounding the O.J. Simpson trial. Personally, I have never treated spouse abuse lightly because I feel that men are cowards who beat helpless and defenseless women. It has been said that in our society, women have called police to their homes and they have been treated with very little dignity by some police officers. Women have said that men just don't get it about spouse abuse. They tend to protect other men.

Women are very vulnerable when they are in these situations because they expect their husbands to be their protectors. Most people have a defect in their personality. They try to demean the other person so that their defect may not be discovered. The most frequently asked question one is asked when people learn that they stayed in an abusive relationship is

"Why did you stay in it?" Many reasons will be given, but the number one answer is insecurity. I will list several steps a person can take to not become a statistic in an abusive relationship.

1. Raise your level of self-esteem by taking self-development courses or by visiting a psychologist to get professional help.

2. Learn to recognize early signs of mental abuse directed toward you from your spouse. (ex. constant put-downs)

3. Keep yourself physically attractive.

4. Get help from trained professionals on spouse abuse.

5. Learn to be honest with yourself.

6. Never alienate yourself from your surrounding family.

7. Talk to your friends about your problems.

8. Develop friends who satisfy your emotional needs.

9. Develop interests not directly related to your spouse to establish your individuality.

10. Never stay in a relationship that is abusive for the sake of your children.

11. Establish a savings account of your own to help you financially get out of an abusive relationship.

12. Ask your spouse to attend family counseling for their abuse.

13. If the abusive party refuses, make plans to get out of the relationship.

Preventing Child Abuse

Our children are the most precious commodity that we have in the world. To see or hear about any child abuse and do nothing is a travesty to mankind. Children cannot protect themselves and it is up to us to provide safety for them. We read in the newspaper and see on TV that many of our children are in serious trouble. Young innocent children in the homes of drug and chemical abuse parents should be watched closely. When they are arrested for various crimes, the children should be taken from them and placed in foster homes or with their relatives. It may sound harsh to take children from their parents, but in many cases it may save their lives. We all remember the incident in North Carolina when the mother drowned her children and told the nation that she did not know where they were. This tragic incident may have been avoided if someone had paid closer attention to the mother and the children. The relatives around children will have to help build a protective net around them.

Social workers will have to do a better job in helping to protect our children. Social workers try to keep children in the home with their parents when the home is in trouble, but if abuse is noticed, the children should be immediately removed from the home. Our laws will have to be changed to protect children who are in abusive homes. Children should only be returned to homes when parents get professional help. After the children return to the homes, they should be monitored by social workers and other officials until parents prove themselves cured of their problem.

School teachers and administrators should help the police spot suspected parents who are abusing their children. Some of the things people might observe about children who may be victims of child abuse are:

1. Children alienating themselves from adults and other children.

2. Children frequently using foul language and cursing.

3. Poor performance in school.

4. Frequent bruises and marks appearing on children.

5. Children telling other children about explicit sexual acts.

6. Children not letting anyone touch them or wanting to receive affection.

7. Bleeding from private parts of children.

8. Children constantly telling you they have something to tell you, but never follow through on it.

When a child's life is suspected to be in jeopardy, any measure someone takes is never a false alarm. We are losing too many kids to child abuse. Many people think that ignoring problems that don't concern them is the way to live. But living is enjoying all forms of life and never wanting to see any form of life destroyed.

Every day in America a child is victimized in some way or another. Listed below are numbers recently reported by the Justice Department on daily crimes against children:

3 children die from abuse or neglect.

6 children commit suicide.

13 children are homicide victims.

15 children are killed by firearms.

95 babies die.

518 babies are born to mothers who had late or no prenatal care.

790 babies are born at low birth weight.

1407 babies are born to teen mothers.

2660 babies are born into poverty.

2833 children drop out of school.

3398 babies are born to unmarried mothers.

6042 children are arrested.

8493 children are reported abused or neglected.

The Justice Department has also reported that crime committed over the internet against children have risen sharply in the last several years. The majority of these crimes are sex solicitations on line. Young adolescents are spending a lot of time on computers because they have their personal computer in their bedroom with unsupervised use. Parents should monitor what their children are doing on the computer especially when they are subscribed to the internet.

There are several web sites to help you keep track of what your children are doing on line that parents can use. If all else fails, simply control a password to monitor when your children are using the internet.

Reducing the Exposure of Violence to Children

Americans are consuming too much violence in their daily lives. Our children are especially learning how to be violent from sports and television. The President and the Senate have talked about the movie industry for not making more television shows and movies suitable for family viewing.

Parents will have to monitor what their children are watching daily on television. Many of the violent movies and TV shows give negative ideas to our children that are later practiced by them. I would be wrong to not say that many parents are teaching their children to be productive members of society. The negative influence from television is still too mind-boggling for many young kids.

Lately, the computer has become the new source of violence for children. Our children are learning information on how to build bombs to blow up buildings and unfortunately sometimes they are the victims themselves. The reason violence sells so well is because of insatiable appetite by the consumer.

Parents should teach their children to walk away from confrontations with other children. If their lives are threatened by another child, report it to the police or other officials. When children try to handle major problems, they usually end up in disaster. If the police are called about children who get their lives threatened, in many cases it can be solved or ended without the loss of life. Children need to be taught that non-violence is the way to handle confrontation. It takes a lot of courage to walk away from potentially violent situations. The anti-violence message from Dr. Martin Luther King, Jr. is hardly ever practiced by our young people. Many adolescents believe carrying a gun makes them a man or woman. We have to start teaching young children to solve problems diplomatically rather than ending them with a weapon. One of the latest violent acts in schools is girls carrying razor blades on their person to slash the faces of other girls. When I first heard this, I said to myself, "How can a girl do this to another girl?" No plastic surgeon can remove those scars from their faces.

It is the job of every parent to teach their children to be good productive citizens and live crime free. If parents do this, it will help to minimize the theory that our young children are lost, being labeled the Generation X. When adolescents end up in prison, they often say that they wish they had been taught better. Others also say, "I wish I had listened to my parents." Either way, the children have to pay for their wrongs. Too many parents are concerned with only their jobs and themselves. They are not concerned enough with raising their children. The more time put in with their children helps reduce their chances of committing crimes and entering the world of crime.

The reason so many kids get into gangs is because they don't feel loved at home. Children have to feel loved and wanted to blossom as caring adults. When you see the run-a-ways in cities, you immediately know something is wrong when children are leaving their homes in large numbers.

When parents know they haven't provided proper guidance and nurturing for their children, they begin to fear them. The fear begins when they notice the violent side of their personality. Can we explain what happens to our children when they make these drastic changes before our eyes? Maybe the answer lies in how we raise our children. Too many parents over compensate for their lack of rearing their children by buying them expensive gifts and showering them with other material things. I don't think it is wrong to give children material things that we may not have had when we were children. But they should be given in a careful moderation so they will appreciate what is done for them. Giving too much to kids too soon only creates a child who thinks he or she has to have everything. When they don't get what they want, many children begin to steal and rob from others.

Recognizing the New Threat to
American Society: "Rage"

Many people in today's society are blaming their conditions on the federal government, employers, and other people. Certainly in today's society things are very competitive in every aspect. Many people are feeling betrayed by the government, employers and other people after loyal devotion to them.

Rage from other people is the new threat to every American regardless of race or economic condition. It may strike at anytime or place when you are around many people. We have all heard of employees who feel that they were wrongfully terminated from their jobs. These disgruntled employees sometime return to their former job and kill their former bosses.

Recognizing rage in people may very well save your life if you are frequently involved with the public. Many of these attacks will be unsuspecting to innocent victims. These attacks represent the lowest form of cowardice a person may see. The following are several ways to recognize rage building in other people and ways to protect yourself:

1. Keep away from people who spew anger at others and employers.

2. Never accept any packages in the mail from people or businesses you do not know.

3. Watch the demeanor of other people without staring.

4. There have been many attacks on innocent people in the news lately but the most tragic is the bombing of the federal building in Oklahoma City, Oklahoma, on April 19, 1995.

Many people in today's society are using their vehicles as weapons on American highways and interstates. Unfortunately, this new form of venting frustration and anger has led to many deaths and serious injuries on roads. Road rage can be sparked on American roads due to discourtesy to other drivers and carelessness of speeding drivers.

To prevent being a victim of road rage, there are certain steps to follow while you are driving on the roads, highways, and interstates.

1. Always drive with courtesy to the other driver.

2. Never follow the car in front of you too closely.

3. Always use your signal lights when you are changing lanes or making turns off the road.

4. Try not to make sudden unknown stops.

5. Never raise your middle finger (giving the bird) to another driver even if the other driver has been rude.

6. Never brandish a weapon to frighten or warn a rude driver.

7. Keep a continuous check on cars coming up behind you in your rearview mirror.

Road rage has become a major problem on American roads and the least infractions you cause while driving may help you save your life from a car crash.

No one can predict negative behavior from other people, but we can do our best to avoid it.

The Types of People Who Commit Crimes

Experts who study the types of people who commit crimes have often said that it is a defect in the personality of the criminal. This is very true and it also may be contributed to the mental state of the person at the time they commit the crime. I don't mean that criminals who commit crimes are insane and insanity should be their primary defense. But we have to look at the character and development of people's lives. The obvious state of crime in America reflects the character of Americans as a whole. In many other countries, crime is not nearly as high as it is in America. One way or another, the American citizen helps to shape the future criminals in our society. Certainly, we are never going to have a society without crime, but progress among the development of people would eliminate most crimes. Our society is deteriorating because crime is so high.

One would certainly have to look at the environment many people live in who commit crimes. If we look at a city like Chicago, per say, more crimes are committed in the inner city than in other parts of the city. Why is this so? It can be contributed to the high rate of unemployment among the residents in the area. The high concentration of drugs in the inner cities is more than in other areas. There are many more other environmental factors to be considered, such as poor housing, education, lack of job skills and the high rate of drug addiction. Many people in the inner cities are law-abiding and have never committed a crime. There are many people who have no desire to commit a crime. I remember going in one of the worst housing projects where I live to assist in transporting low income residents without transportation to the polls to vote in the local government election. I approached an apartment surrounded by other apartments that were dilapidated and had the appearance of a slum environment. The apartment that I was going to to pick up a resident was different, to say the least. It had pretty flowers on the front porch and a welcome mat. I knocked on the door and a lady of about forty-five came to the door smiling with a warm personality. She invited me in to her home for a minute to finish gathering her personal things to leave. When I came in to her home, I forgot that I was in a low-income housing project because it was so neat and clean in appearance. Everything was neatly arranged and well-kept. I remember that her furniture was not all new, but coordinated in detail colors. As we left the apartment and was traveling back to the place to vote, I could not help but to tell her that her apartment was very impressive. I told her how neat and clean it was and that most people are wrong to assume that all residents lived like animals in housing projects. She was very pleased with my compliments and softly smiled.

Now many people like her are trapped in an environment that is conducive to criminal behavior and still maintain their dignity. If all children in housing projects had a mother like the lady I met, crime would be kept to a minimum in those areas.

What about people who come from non-poverty stricken areas who commit crimes? How can you explain the behavior of well-adjusted people who commit crimes? In 1988, a white male General Motors executive was fired from his job and could not find another one to replace his six figure income. When the mortgage company was about to foreclose on his home, he went out and robbed three banks to pay off his home. When he felt that he was going to lose his lifestyle, the only answer that came to him was to rob a bank to maintain his level of living. Many people in low-income areas live daily under the threat of foreclosure and never think of robbing banks.

Crime is often committed by desperate people who do not see a way out of a hardship at a present time. Individuals have to be taught at an early age about character development and live honest, clean lives. The reasons many people are committing crimes are needs for material things. When they can't get the things that are so appealing to them on television, they rob and steal for them. Others commit crimes to finance their drug addiction. The black population has the highest crime rate for the simple need for material things. Most of the crimes are committed against fellow residents of their same neighborhoods. The Willie Horton Fear Theory among whites was manifested to get the white votes in the Republican Party. The fact is most blacks commit crimes against other blacks and most whites commit crime against other whites.

Racism is the common factor behind many crimes in the black community. Although many blacks have persevered and became productive citizens, racism is still behind the high crime rate in the black communities. The unemployment rate is too high among young black males who are falling prey to criminal activity. Many young blacks desperately want to work but can't find jobs. The self-esteem is crushed among many black males and they have developed a "get paid" philosophy, meaning if you won't let them work for it, they will take it. The instinct for a man to survive is primary among any man as well as it is among other animals. When the dignity of a man is taken, you are dealing with disaster. Many young blacks know what they are doing is wrong, but they contribute their crimes to the oppression they face from day to day racism.

We are moving to a society of the haves and have nots. Politicians are catering to the wealthy and paying little attention to the poor. If this trend continues, we will always have a high rate of crime in our society. The well-to-do will have to build iron gates around their neighborhoods and hire security guards to keep the criminals out.

Individuals can do several things to correct some of the wrongs they see in their neighborhoods and in society. When a person knows of criminal behavior in a neighborhood, they must report it to the police. Crimes are like fires, the bigger they get, the harder they are to put out.

In 2009, two judges were charged with illegally jailing adolescents and for receiving $2.6 million in kickback fraud schemes. The juvenile offenders were brought before the judges without a lawyer, denied due process, and then sent off to prison for minor offenses. The reason the juveniles were illegally jailed because two privately-run detention centers wanted to warehouse the youths and receive contracts totally more than $58 million. The judges had been practicing for at least twelve years. The judges agreed to plead guilty to the crimes in federal court and could receive more than seven years in prison.

How can one explain the fact that two white judges with very comfortable incomes risk their careers for crimes that could be easily detected. The answer is simple—greed, and everyone has a capacity to commit crimes from any race or background.

In 2009, the American Broadcasting Company (ABC) did a story on poverty, joblessness, drugs, and crime in the hills of Appalachia, Kentucky. The selling of prescription drugs was reported as the number one income producer for many of the unskilled residents in Appalachia. Because of the high

unemployment rate in Appalachia, many people did not

apologize for selling drugs. The people in Appalachia are 99.9%

white, and all of the factors that support why crimes is a problem

in all communities have similar problems like Appalachia.

Dealing With Youths in Gangs

Youths in gangs are terrorizing neighborhoods all over the country. The mere thought of mentioning gangs are in any neighborhood brings immediate fear to residents. The gang problem has gotten so bad that many police forces have started gang task units. It is very hard to deal with gangs once they are established.

The most preventable measures anyone can take to prevent gang-related crimes are to keep kids from joining gangs. Many children who join gangs are runaways but they also come from homes with one or both parents in the home. Parents need to pay close attention to their children in their early formative years to keep them from joining gangs. The most important thing that has to be taught to kids to keep them out of gangs is individualism. Children have to be taught that they have their own personality and do not need to copy others. Parents have to teach their children leadership skills so that when they are confronted about joining gangs they can say no. I realize saying no to some of them won't make a difference. But if kids are harassed to join gangs, they should contact the police and report

the harasser. Children also need to be taught to ask for their

parents' help if they are being harassed. Most of the time when

children try to confront gangs alone it usually ends in disaster.

Teaching Your Children to Protect Themselves From Being Abducted, Molested, and Sexually Abused

I have said in an earlier chapter that our children are the most important things that we have in our world. So we must protect them and teach them how to protect themselves from potential criminals. We assume that our children are too young when they are preschool age to tell them certain things about life in general. Teaching our children very early about crime and the personality of criminals can save their lives. Our children are being abducted daily because they do not take precautions when strangers approach them. Even if children know to not get in a car with a stranger, they may be lured in if they don't think instinctively about protecting themselves. Listed are several things that parents should teach their children at an early age from being abducted.

1.   Children should never talk to strangers or maintain eye contact with someone who is trying to talk to them.

2.   Children should never get in the car with anyone, unless it has been pre-approved by a parent. Many

80

children are abducted and killed by someone they know.

3.   Teach your children to not wear loose clothing so they cannot be easily grabbed by someone.

4.   If someone asks a child to play with a pet, teach them to say that their parents do not want them to play with other people's pets.

5.   Tell your children to not accept any gifts from someone they do not know.

6.   Children should be taught if they are touched inappropriately by anyone, they should tell a parent, teacher, minister or anyone else in authority.

7.   Children should never be allowed to open the doors at home to strangers.

8.   Parents should always open the doors to their home when they are at home.

9.   Teach your children to tell adults, even if they are school administrators, they should not be in a room alone with them.

Children do not have fears formed at an early age and should be taught to fear things that may harm them. The sooner kids are taught to fear being abducted, the better they will be able to protect themselves.

Harvesting Organs From Live Humans

Many people have life-threatening illnesses that require having an organ transplanted in their body. The population is growing for people who are waiting on transplants. Very few people are donating organs to help the increasingly needy population waiting for transplants. Because of this limited supply of available organs, many people who have wealth are turning to underworld people who sell organs for profit. These underworld people obtain organs by any means necessary.

One example of how these people get organs is by slipping a knockout drug in an unsuspecting patron's glass in a bar. The drug may have the person out for several hours. An experienced medical person then comes to where you have been taken and retrieves an organ from you. Usually, the organ thieves will take your (ex. kidney), and leave you in a hotel bathtub packed in ice. A note may accompany you advising you not to move because your kidney has been harvested and you should immediately call an ambulance or other medical professionals.

This may seem like something from a science fiction movie, but it is happening in today's society. Because of the nature of this crime, you may never or the law ever find the person or persons who did this to you. The best way to prevent this happening to you is:

1. Never go into a bar that you are not familiar with alone.

2. Never leave your drink unattended in a bar.

3. Beware of people who are getting too personal with you.

4. Never drink to become incapacitated.

5. Above all, always be very careful.

Preventing Credit Card Usage Theft

Credit card usage theft has become a major problem since we have come into the computer age. People are paying by credit cards for all types of purchases, big or small. Probably the only way to prevent credit card usage theft is to limit the purchases you make by phone. A credit card should never be used to purchase items over the television, radio, and other media. A person who obtains your number for a product can easily use your credit card for another purchase since he or she knows your number. You may not know about the purchase until you receive your bill. If you want to purchase a product you hear about over the media, you should always pay by check. You should deposit cash into your checking account to write a check. Credit cards should only be used when you are making a purchase in person. Gasoline and phone credit cards are relatively safe unless they are stolen.

If your credit card is stolen you should immediately report it to the police. If your card is lost, you should report it to the credit card maker.

Credit card purchases are always risky over the internet and should be used with caution.

The Future of Crime Fighting
Among Law Enforcement

We all wish that we could live in a society that is crime free. But unfortunately we know that this will never be. What does the future hold for fighting crime in our society? Technology has advanced in many areas of our society including law enforcement. One of the most common advancements we learned about was during the O.J. Simpson trial. DNA was introduced to the world during the trial.

In 1990, DNA was also used to capture a man in California who was convicted of killing six women. The killer would stalk his potential victims outside a health club and follow them to their homes. The police found some of his semen and was later able to match his DNA with the semen. The killer would have never been caught if DNA was not used.

Listed below are other new crime-fighting techniques used by law enforcement officers.

1. Infrared cameras are being mounted on cars to catch suspects at night.

2. Video cameras are mounted in police cars to videotape potential suspects.

3. Infrared lighting mechanisms are mounted on helicopters to follow suspects on foot and in cars.

4. Police officers will use infrared night vision goggles to find suspects at night.

5. Computerized virtual reality training scenarios are used to train police officers.

6. Road spikes will be used to stop fleeing automobiles on highways and interstates.

7. Remote control devices will be used to place under moving automobiles to disable their electrical systems in a chase.

8. Police will use nets launched by a machine to stop fleeing suspects.

9. A belt called a "react belt" will be used to disable suspects who try to run away from police when they are in custody.

10. Heavy sticky glue shot from a gun to stop suspect from fleeing a scene.

11. A gun has been invented to shoot hard rubber balls at suspects to stop them from fleeing instead of killing them.

12. A bullet called a "composite bullet" shot from guns that will not ricochet when aimed at a target.

13. Robots will be used to disarm bombs instead of using police officers.

14. Robots will be used to enter buildings when armed suspects are in them.

15. A computerized instrument will be used to identify bomb components of bombs used in crimes.

16. Law enforcement will use guns that will be able to fire only by the officers. The officers will wear a ring that will enable the gun to be only fired by the officer. If the criminal takes the gun away in a struggle, he will not be able to fire it.

Using Automatic Teller Machines (ATM's) Carefully

Automatic Teller Machines (ATMs) are being used frequently in today's fast-paced society. People are using ATMs because of long lines in the bank and quick access to money. A customer at an ATM should be extremely careful when using them. Criminals target ATMs because they are rarely guarded by security and often not in public places.

Listed are several ways to protect yourself when using ATMs.

1. Never use ATMs that are not well-lighted.

2. Never go into a housed ATM with other people in it.

3. Use only ATMs in malls and heavy traffic areas when possible.

4. If you are attacked while using an ATM, throw the money out of the car or away from you and speed or run away.

5. Never count your money while still parked at an ATM.

Recognizing Scams

Scam artists in our society today are nothing new to the world of crime. There have been many scams pulled on innocent victims because they have never heard of the particular scam. I have heard of many scams, but the one that I was suckered into was one called "stuffing envelopes" for profit. About ten years ago, I read an ad in the local newspaper advertising that you can make extra money stuffing envelopes with information for profit. The ad suggested that you would be paid by the number of envelopes you stuffed. I saw this ad as an excellent opportunity to make more money right out of my home. To purchase the starter kit, you had to send $49.95 to get started. I rushed to the post office and sent my money to the address listed in the ad. About a week later, I received a reply from the placer of the ad suggesting that I must be a fool to think that someone would pay me to stuff envelopes by hand when there are machines that can stuff hundreds of envelopes every minute. Obviously, I was outdone by being taken, but even more for being naïve. I said to myself that I should have known better. But since that incident, I have learned to call the Better Business Bureau before sending any money to someone that I know nothing about.

There are many scams out there and I am listing some with their descriptions.

1.   Pigeon Drop Scam

This scam is presented to you by two strangers who suggest that they have found a bag of money and want to share it with you. You are then asked to go and get a sum suggested by the scammers out of your account to put up as good faith money. The scam artist takes your money and tells you they are going to their car to count the money. Once they leave, you will never see them or your money again.

2.   Pyramid Schemes

These scams work because many people desperately want to start their own business by joining these groups. Once you are in the group, you will make a small amount of money far less than the amount of time you have put in. The person who starts the pyramid scheme gets rich off you and others. Most of the time pyramid schemes collapse after a few years.

3. Law Enforcement Funds

You are called by telephone to help law enforcement people raise money for various causes. The solicitor will tell you to send the money to an organization or want you to place it on your credit card. If you suspect fraud from a caller requesting money to be sent to a law enforcement agency, be sure to get the full name of the caller. If the caller is a fraud, he or she will hang up.

4. Fire Alarm Sales People

Many people are selling door to door alarms to warn you against smoke and fire. The alarms usually cost thousands of dollars. Don't be fooled because you can buy a smoke and fire alarm from any major department store for about twenty dollars apiece.

5. Credit Repair Fraud

These ads are usually placed in newspapers suggesting that your credit can be repaired or restored for a fee. No one other than you and the creditor can work out a resolution to restore your credit.

6. Employment Ads

These ads promise you jobs if you send money to the placer of the ad. They tell you they will guarantee you a job in America or overseas for your fee. No one can guarantee that you will be hired by a company.

7. Buying Jewelry on the Street

Do not ever buy jewelry on the street from anyone. Many times the jewelry is either stolen or worthless.

8. Fortune Telling Frauds

People are vulnerable to quick fixes of their lives calling mind readers and fortune tellers. When you call or visit these people, you will be giving your money away for general information.

9. False Prophets

Many false preachers are asking you to send money to their organizations to pray for you. After they get you hooked into sending money, they want to keep you sending money monthly.

10. Professional Career Agents

These agents promise you that they will jump-start your professional careers. Many of these people promise young people careers in acting, singing and other professions only if they pay money to them. Most of these people provide you with nothing and keep draining your money from you.

11. Baby Adoption Scams

Baby adoption scams are taking money from unsuspecting want-a-be parents and never providing babies to them. One must only deal with people who have excellent references for adopting children.

12. Christmas Charities Scams

Christmas time scams are very easy to pull off because many people are in gift-giving moods. Be aware of scams during Christmas time.

13. Sale of Non-Trademark Merchandise

Many people are selling non-trademark merchandise on the street and in stores. Some of the items sold are fake Gucci bags and Nike merchandise. A person who is purchasing these items should be able to recognize the trademarks before the purchase.

14. The Water Filter Scam

People are going around to homes in neighborhoods asking to check your drinking water for $40 to $60 to see if it is safe. When they get a vile of tap water from you to test, it is switched with a vile that is contaminated. The scam artist then tells you to purchase a drinking water purifier for about two thousand dollars. If someone comes to your home to test your water, simply tell them you will have the city test your water.

15. Weight Loss Pills

Many of these pills are advertised on television and in magazines. These pills are simply water reduction methods for your body and you will gain the weight back when you stop taking them. Some of these pills are unsafe.

16. Car Repair Fraud

Most women are victims of car repair fraud, but it can happen to anyone. Innocent victims are over-charged for car repair and many times charged for services not done.

The best way to avoid car repair fraud is to get a second opinion. Another way to avoid car repair fraud is to buy repair insurance to be honored by certified mechanics.

17. Diamond Jewelry Switching

Scam artists switch jewelry being shown during sale demonstrations with cubic Zirconia. Cubic Zirconia looks like a real diamond to the naked eyes. Jewelry sales people should never take their eyes off the store jewelry when being shown.

18. Taxi-Driver Scam

Many taxi drivers in large cities take advantage of out-of-town people who are not familiar with cities they are visiting. Taxi drivers drive all around the destination to run up fares on unsuspecting out-of-town people.

19. Insurance Policy Scam

Insurance agents many times sell worthless policies to old people without a conscious. Before a person signs an insurance policy, he or she should let someone who knows about insurance look over the policy.

20. Parking Attendant Scam

Scam artists usually surround large events such as ball games or rock concerts to collect money from you to park your car. Many of these people collect your money and do not own the property they are pretending to own. Your vehicle may be towed away when you return. Always park your vehicle in locations authorized by the event staff or park in locations where you have direct knowledge of the property.

21. Cable Box Scam

Cable boxes are sold to individuals suggesting that you can receive pay channels directly from the unauthorized cable box. Don't be deceived because these cable boxes do not descramble codes from your local cable company.

22. Used Car Sale Fraud

Sometimes the mileage has been rolled back on used cars being sold. If you are purchasing a used car from an individual or dealer, ask to see the service history on the car. If the miles and the maintenance are in question, do not purchase the vehicle.

23. Money Investment Scam

Beware of people who try to get you to invest in risky money-making adventures. If the deals seem too good to be true, then they are probably not good investments. Most business deals are bad if you rush into them. Some of these other money investment scams are:

1. Work at home scams that require you to send money to start your business.

2. Investment Scams

    A. Gas Wells

    B. Oil Wells

    C. Land

    D. Livestock

    E. Prize (Won) Scams

3. They ask you to send money to receive your prize.

    A. Receiving Free Grant Money

4. Envelope Stuffing

    A. Requires you to send the same information you received for your money to someone else to get money in return.

5. Recovery Room Scam

    A. Requires you to send money to recovery room to

    recover money you have lost in scam.

6. Avoid Foreign Lotteries

    A. Foreign lotteries are illegal.

7. Charities

    A. Check out charities by calling the Better Business

    Bureau. Never give on the spur of the moment.

You may not remember all the scams out there, but look and

listen for these red flags.

1. You've been specially selected to hear this offer.

2. You've won a valuable prize.

3. This investment is low risk, high return.

4. You must make up your mind right now.

You don't need to know about every scam out there, but

you need to be suspicious of any caller or items received in the

mail. Listed are certain things you need to know.

1. Ask questions

    A. Ask for the name of the caller and the name of the

    company he or she works for. Often times the

phone caller is working off a prepared script. When you ask questions, you will probably confuse him or her.

2. Make sure telemarketers don't violate the telemarketing sales rule. The telemarketers must call between 8:00 am and 9:00 p.m. They must tell you it's a sales call and reveal their company's name. If it is a prize promotion, they must tell you that you don't have to purchase anything or pay money to win.

3. It's illegal for a company to call a second time if you have asked them to place you on the "do not call" list. Write down the date and the time that you have asked to be put on the "do not call" list. Also ask for the person's name that you are speaking to.

Some other ways to protect yourself are:

1. Take your time making decisions—sleep on it.

2. Do your homework; call the Better Business Bureau.

3. Don't give your credit card, checking account or social security number out to anyone over the phone or through the mail.

4. Don't send cash by courier or overnight mail. If you send cash, you might lose your right to dispute fraudulent charges.

5. If you are very uncomfortable with a caller, simply hang up the phone.

24. Computer Information Scams

The computer age will bring many uses to homes using personal computers. Unfortunately, there will be many scams pulled over the computer as there are over the phone. Be careful about sending money for products or information on computer phone lines.

On March 7, 2009, I received a check for $2,000.00 for an item I had advertised on the internet for $180.00. The person who answered the ad sent a $2,000.00 check and wanted me to cash it, then take $180.00 for the item and send the remainder to a third party by Western Union.

I took the check to the bank to verify its authenticity. The bank stated it was fraudulent and reported it to the fraud unit. If you receive a suspected fraudulent check made out to you, do not take it to a teller window. Give the check to management personnel so that they will not

suspect you are a part of the fraud.

The check and the third party information is shown below.

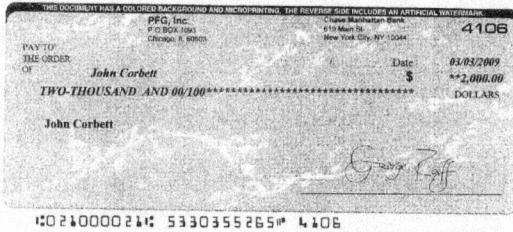

INSTRUCTIONS:

When you receive this check, email me at jbinstructions@aol.com and tell me that
you received the check. Then get the check cashed in your bank, deduct your
funds and wire the excess funds to the following information via Western Union
only.

Ellen Lewis
Washington, DC 20002
United States

Email me immediately after you wire the money with the following information:

- Senders name and address
- Western Union MTCN
- Amount sent after the Western Union fees

Please do not wire funds via Money Gram, we do not accept that.
Funds should not be sent/wired to United Kingdom because we have temporarily
close down our United Kingdom office to avoid Internet fraud, Email us
immediately at jbinstructions@aol.com so that we can report this fraud If anyone
directs you to wire the funds to any other information, or United Kingdom or via
Money Gram, please notify me immediately. Unknown account wire transfers will
be at your own risk.

Thank you!

On March 29, 2009, I received an e-mail entitled "Urgent Business Proposal" from a person posing as a government official in Johannesburg, South Africa. The solicitor was requesting my assistance to transfer $25,000,000 (twenty-five million dollars) to a United States bank from his investments in South Africa. He further stated that he could not keep the sizable amount in a bank in South Africa because of the unstable political environment.

I phoned the Better Business Bureau on March 31, 2009 to explain the e-mail. The Better Business Bureau confirmed that this was an e-mail scam and stated that there were thousands more circulating over the internet similar to this one.

The common link in the scam is that the sender wants you to deposit money in a bank to receive your commission. One of the noticeable things that raised a red flag about this e-mail was that the sender did not correctly spell Johannesburg in the address heading.

The proposed letter is listed on the next page.

From:	"Mr. George Poyser" <gesr758@gmail.com>	Sent: Sun 03/29/09 8:59 PM
To:		Priority: Normal
Subject:	FINANCE $ ECONOMIC AFFAIRS DEPT. (SOUTH AFRICA)	

DEPARTMENT OF FINANCE & ECONOMIC AFFAIRS
JOHANNEBURG,SOUTH AFRICA
Tel: +27-833614479
Email: georgepsr758@gmail.com

Dear Sir/Madam

URGENT BUSINESS PROPOSAL

After my official enquiry from the foreign trade office of the chambers of commerce & industry here in Johannesburg South Africa, I decided to contact you but I did not disclose the intention to anyone else because of the delicate nature of the project.

I found your profile very interesting and decided to reach you directly to solicit for your assistance and guidelines in making a business investment and transfer of US$25,000,000.00(Twenty Five Million Dollars) to your country within the next few days. Please I must plead for your confidence in this transaction.

I am a high placed official working with Department of (Finance & Economic Affairs) in Johannesburg. I and two other colleagues are currently in need of a silent foreign partner whose identity we can use to transfer this sum of money. But at this moment, I am constrained to issue more details about this profitable business investment until I get your response by email, please if you can take out a moment of your very busy schedule today to respond back to my private email below for more details and include your private telephone number in your response which I and my colleagues will highly appreciate.

This fund accrued legitimately to us as commission from foreign contracts, through our private connections. The fund is presently waiting to be remitted from the bank here in South Africa to any overseas beneficiary confirmed by us as associate/receiver. By virtue of our positions as civil servants in my country, we cannot acquire this money in our names. Because as high placed civil servants, we are not allowed by the civil service code of conduct to own or operate bank accounts outside of our shores.

On the other hand, it is not safe for us to keep the money here due to unstable political environment. I have been mandated as a matter of trust by my colleagues, to look for an overseas silent partner who could work with us to facilitate transfer of this fund for our mutual benefit, Hence the reason for this email.

My proposal is that after you receive the funds, it would be shared as follows: (1) 15% to you as commission for your co-operation and assistance in facilitating the transfer, while the remaining 85% belongs to me and two colleagues. You will be free to take out your commission immediately after the money hits your account in your country.

Since our objective is to invest the money in a foreign country, it would be appreciated if you could also help us with advices and direction on investing into profitable ventures in your country. However, this is optional, and if it is not convenient for you to further assist us with investing the money, we can end our cooperation after you make available to me our part of the money.

The transaction, although discreet, is legitimate and the money will be transferred successfully with all necessary back-up official documents showing the legitimate source/origin of fund. The transfer will be effected within a period not longer than two weeks as soon as we reach an agreement and you furnish me with a suitable response indicating your interest for processing the transfer.
I plead with you on one issue, whether you are interested or not, kindly do not expose this information to any one else. I confirm that the transaction is legitimate and without any risks either to us or yourself. Please, give me your response immediately by returning this mail through my alternative email address.
georgepsr758@gmail.com
Mr. George Poyser
Finance & Economic Affairs Dept. (South Africa)

25. Cruise Ship Scams

Many travel agencies advertise terrific deals on cruise ship vacations, but they don't tell you the whole story. Sometimes cruise ship vacation offers do not provide transportation to and from ship dock. Some deals may be the room and board only and you have to pay for the food.

26. Chain Letter scams

A letter is mailed to your address suggesting if you don't put money in an envelope and mail it, you will have evil and bad things to happen to you. However, if you follow the instructions and mail money with the letter, you have been definitely scammed.

27. Checking Account Scam

People will call your home and tell you that you have won a prize from their company. In order to collect your prize, you are asked to give out your checking account number to debit your account for the prize. Once you receive the prize, you will see that the prize costs far less than the money debited from your checking account. Never give out your checking account number to anyone over the phone.

28. Vending Machine Business Investment Scam

Vending machines are sold in the classified ads as a business investment. Many of these companies are selling poorly-manufactured machines that take money and do not dispense a product. Many times people will spend more money than the machines are worth after they are repaired.

Only buy vending machines that are demonstrated in person and have good warranties.

29. Credit Card Fraud Scams

Criminals are assuming the identity of people who hold credit cards with high spendable limits. Impostors select potential victims from credit reports and mailing lists that can be purchased from information-providing companies. In today's society, there are many electronic devices produced on the market to help escalate crimes that make a lot of money for criminals. One electronics device that has been created is a machine that duplicates the numbers and codes on your credit cards. The device is very small so that it can be carried in your pocket anywhere you go. One example of how people use the device is when you give your credit card to someone to pay for your purchase in a store or out to dinner. The clerk or waiter may take your card out of your viewing area and run your card through the illegal card swiping machine just like the legal card swiping machine to gain the information from the card. Once the thief has stolen your information from your card, he or she can go home and make a card identical to your card and transfer the information to their card. Then, he or she has unlimited purchases to deplete your money limit to zero dollars. You won't know your money is gone until you receive your bill. This new credit card theft is almost never prosecuted because the person can say that you gave them your card to make the purchases. The purchases would probably have been made long before you could report the card stolen.

The only way you can prevent someone from stealing the information from your cards is to not let someone take your credit card out of your viewing area to pay for your purchases. If someone takes your card out of your viewing area, simply tell them you want to see the store credit card machine being used to make your purchases.

In 2008, federal regulators adopted new rules that will go into effect in July 2010 which will allow credit card companies to raise interest rates only on new credit cards and future purchases or advances, rather than on current balances. The reason for the changes is because banks have been raising interest rates at high levels, defrauding their customers. Even people with excellent credit records have been defrauded. The new rules prohibit:

- Placing unfair time constraints on payments. A payment could not be deemed late unless the borrower is given a reasonable period of time, such as 21 days, to pay.

- Placing too-high fees for exceeding the credit limit solely because of a hold placed on the account.

- Unfairly computing balances in a computing tactic knows are double-cycle billing.

- Unfairly adding security deposits and fees for issuing credit or making it available.

- Making deceptive offers of credit.

    Under new rules, credit card lenders will be required to apply any payment above the minimum to the part of the balance with the highest interest rate.

    The so-called subprime cards for people with low credit scores typically have no more than a $500 credit limit but require a larger up front fee.

This information was reported by an Associated Press business writer, Marcy Gordon, on December 18, 2008.

Credit card number stealing over the internet is also a new crime that is pulled off by a hacker who enters the files of a business and steals credit card numbers. The hacker can steal all credit card numbers for purchases over the internet and demand blackmail money for the safe return of the credit card numbers.

30. <u>Identity Theft</u>

This is a form of theft where a person can retrieve information on you from your discarded garbage. Thieves can use this information on you that they have found to make credit cards, social security cards, and other identification. The identification is sold to people who may have entered the country illegally to find work. A thief who finds your information from your garbage on bank accounts, credit card limits and other assets may duplicate cards to take all of your money from your accounts.

Medical ID theft is one of the new growing leading frauds because the medical costs have skyrocketed. People don't really think about or consider that medical information is the new target for thieves. One man's medical ID was stolen and used to rent a medical helicopter for transport at a cost of $19,000. You should always tear up or shred your bills and other information related to medical. Being a victim of medical ID theft can lead on to:

- Bankruptcy

- Bad credit reports

- Your medical information changed

- Enormous bills billed to you at your expense

31. Theft By Diversion

This theft is pulled off by many people entering a business at one time to create a diversion so that the clerk cannot watch everyone at one time. Several people in the diversion may divert the clerk's attention so that others can enter the office to steal large sums of money or take money from the open cash register. The store clerk may not know that the theft has occurred until the store has been cleared of all persons. After viewing a video camera, you may be able to see how the theft has occurred. But if you don't have a video camera working to help identify thieves, you may never be able to recover your loss.

32. Unsolicited E-mail

Many people are going online on the computer to send harassing and stalking e-mails to unsuspecting receivers. Most of these offenders are probably known by their offenders and probably live in their own community. The best way to protect yourself is to be careful who you give your e-mail address to. There is very little a person can do to stop this crime from occurring because of the varied use of the computer. One of the best ways to protect yourself is to subscribe to an internet provider who has very good security.

33. Illegal Internet Web Sites

Over 116,000 businesses on the internet are soliciting for money illegally and don't deliver on goods that are being bought. They take your money from you quickly because most customers will not want to check the web sites out with agencies like the Better Business Bureau.

34. Internet Cyber-Stalkers

Many people are conversing with people on the internet that they know nothing about. These people may plan to stalk you by buying personal information about you. After they know your daily routine, they will stalk you with intentions of later harming you. Tips for protecting yourself against cyber stalkers are:

1. Use software to block unwanted harassing e-mails from entering your computer.

2. Go online with your children to see what they are receiving.

3. Report any offensive material received to your internet provider.

4. Above all, use caution with any person who is a stranger to you.

35. Lottery Ticket Scams

In states where lottery tickets are sold, some people may try to convince you that they have won a sizable amount in the lottery drawing and they are holding the winning ticket. They may tell you that they are not United States citizens and cannot claim the prize money but want to give you a part of the winnings and ask you to turn in the ticket for the bogus winning. When you try to turn in the lottery ticket for the prize money, you are told that the ticket is a fraud.

36. Internet Car Sales Frauds

People will try to scam you by telling you they are moving to a foreign country and have to sell their car because it is too expensive to ship it. They will say they will buy a car when they get to their destination. They want you to wire them half of the drastically reduced sale of the car because they are in the country trying to get settled and do not have the time to price negotiate. They want the money wired to a third party to try to distance themselves from the scam. However way they present the fraud to you, you will be taken because it will be virtually impossible to get your money back.

37. Car Auction Sale Frauds

Most frauds at car auctions are committed at auctions opened to the public. Anyone can register a car and sell it at these auctions once they pay a fee to the auctioneer.

Most of the owners of these cars will not be honest with you
and tell you exactly what's wrong with their car. Many of
the cars may have internal engine or transmission problems.
Some cars may have been pieced together from junk yards.
These cars are sold with no money-back guarantee.

38. Identify Theft Using the Internet

Some people are sending e-mails stating that you have
received a refund from the Internal Revenue Service due to
you. The e-mail further states that you must send personal
information about yourself in order to retrieve the refund.
The personal information may then be used to make
purchases on your name and access financial accounts that
may belong to you.

39. Companies Who Scam You and Other Companies

Many companies use dishonest tactics in operating their
businesses every day. If they are never caught, they call
their practices simply good business. All companies do not
practice dishonest policies, but there are many that do. A
customer will never know when they have been scammed
because they don't know the correct practices of a

company. It will simply be up to the company to practice good ethics.

Employees who see the violations practiced and scams against customers have a duty to act to correct the problems they see. People can win large awards by whistleblowing on their employers for unlawful practices. There have been many whistleblowers against companies since the law came into effect.

40. Second Mortgage Scams

Many people get second mortgages to repair, add on to their existing property, or use the money to buy other things. The purchaser of the second mortgage may not know that the interest will balloon or they might lose their home because they did not understand the fine print.

41. Work at Home Scams

There are many people scamming others by telling them they can work at home and make good money doing it. There are many of these scams out there, but two of the most popular are stuffing envelopes and medical billing.

42. Automobile Warranty Scams

Car repairs have gotten so high that many people are buying automobile warranties from solicitors in the mail. They simply ask you to send the payment through the mail to cover specific areas of your car.

43. Vanity Award Scam

An e-mail message is sent informing an organization that it has been selected for an award. The e-mail message, sent from the U.S. Local Business Association in Washington, DC, gives you the option of buying a plaque. But once you fill out the information on your business profile, you can't find out what the plaque will cost. The scammer is basically gathering information on you to be sold to a third party.

44. Home Foreclosure Scams

People are calling home owners telling them they have a plan to rescue their home from foreclosure. The tip-off that it is a scam is when they ask for your money for the plan up front.

45. Slave Reparations Scam

The Internal Revenue Service is warning blacks to be aware

of people telling them that they can receive tax credits or

refunds related to slave reparations if they give the scammer

money.

How to Avoid Being a Victim of a Scam

The old saying, if it is too good to be true, then it usually is, is the best way to keep yourself in check from being scammed.

One would have to think why is a complete stranger wanting to help or share something with you when they don't even know you. People get hooked by many people because of greed and trusting others too much. The best way to keep yourself from being scammed is to not make rash decisions. Train yourself to think about a decision before you make anything final.

Almost everyone will be scammed at some point in their lifetime. It is virtually impossible to not be scammed by someone because there are so many scams being used on people that it will be virtually impossible to know them all.

Another way to keep from being scammed is to ask questions about the transaction or situation. Most people will want to run from you when you ask probing questions because they will make them uncomfortable.

Preventing Dishonest Repair Service People From Victimizing You in Your Home

Elderly people are being victimized by dishonest repair service people daily. These types of criminals prey on an individual's fear and their moments of weakness. They take advantage of people by saying that an appliance may be putting their lives in danger when they are in fact not. The best way to protect yourself against dishonest repair service people is to always get a second opinion on a repair job. Repair service people also try to get you to buy a new appliance when you may not need one.

One of the most common scams used on people who need their air conditioning or heating units serviced is done from the parent offices. In northern cities where the temperatures get very low, dishonest repair service people create more wrongs to the heating unit than are present.

Contractors will take advantage of you when you are building or making repairs to your home if you are not knowledgeable about what they are supposed to be doing. When you hire a contractor for work, make sure that everything he or she is to do is itemized on the work order. Make sure that the cost of materials is listed along with the estimated hours to complete the work. Never partially pay for work completed before the overall job is finished unless you and the contractor have agreed on payment for services on a given date. Ask the city inspector to come out to the work site to check to see if the work is being done properly. Also ask the city inspector to check the quality of materials being used.

Many people are relaxed about business deals and think that no one will take advantage of them. Unfortunately, there are many dishonest people who appear to be very honest. The average customer does not know they are ignorant of what to expect.

The Criminal Population

Most crimes are committed by men in America and throughout the world. Only a small amount of crimes are committed by women. The ratio of murders committed in America is six men to every one woman, for assault, seven to one, robbery, twenty-two to one and burglary, thirty to one. The vast difference between male and female criminals is that women tend to commit crimes in isolation rather than in the company of a group. Shoplifting is the number one crime for women. Most men commit crimes in a group. In the case of violent crimes, women tend to commit most of them upon members of their own family.

The age of offenders committing crimes is frequently under age twenty-five. A lot of kids dabble in crimes such as shoplifting while teenagers but never advance to more serious crimes. These crimes are committed as a result of peer pressure. For many young adults, the threat of incarceration is enough of a deterrent to not lead a life of crime. The more serious crimes such as homicide are committed by people who are twenty-five years and older.

Most crimes in the United States indicate a higher rate for blacks than whites over a wide range of offenses. A lot of crimes committed by blacks are in direct proportion to crack cocaine in their neighborhood. The sentencing for crack cocaine is far greater for blacks than whites who use white powder cocaine. White powder cocaine is found more often in affluent white neighborhoods. Many times, the white users of powder cocaine are given the option to enter pre-trial diversion programs before they even go to trial. The high rate of white-collar crimes is rarely reported to the news media. Blacks have less opportunity to commit these crimes because they do not have access to high corporate level jobs. The discriminatory attitude of law enforcement is more prone to arrest blacks and counsel whites. Blacks are more predisposed to crime in ghettos. The ghetto subculture is a breeding ground for criminal activity among many blacks. The vast majority of crimes committed by blacks are committed against other blacks, not against whites.

Other explanations of the high crime rate among blacks in the United States relates to the vicious cycle in job discrimination. Black unemployment is twice as high as unemployment among whites. Other minority groups have high unemployment rates, but not as high as blacks.

Whites commit the majority of their crimes against other whites. No one group of people has a monopoly on crimes. If each race of people is given the same set of circumstances, most people would handle the circumstances the same.

Gun Control

The debate over serious gun control by the federal government will go on until the end of time of man. A logically thinking person can easily analyze that there is a serious connection between unregistered guns on the street and crime. The fear of many citizens is that they believe that if gun control is legislated, it would mean that they would ultimately have to give up their gun. They believe that this would not be consistent with the constitutional right to bear arms. Both sides of the gun control debate have valid arguments. The only way many people will change their views on gun control is to be directly affected by a crime committed against them with a gun.

The most persuasive reason for stiffer gun control was witnessed by many Americans in the late 1990's. We will never forget the many senseless acts of random violence that occurred in our schools over and over again. It was like a nightmare that continued to appear again and again. But this was not a dream but reality. The saddest fact that these students committed these awful crimes came from households who worshipped the use of guns in their daily lives. Many of them never thought that teaching their children to include the use of guns in their lives would come back to haunt them. This is certainly not to say that kids who are raised around guns will commit murder or other crimes. Statistics will show that the majority of children raised around guns have never and will never commit a crime.

Certainly another factor around gun control should be the psychological state of the person who owns a gun. It certainly would not be a bad idea to make gun owners take psychological tests periodically to see if they are stable enough to own a gun. There also could be many other ways to monitor and control people who own guns. But in our society, we wait until something awful happens and then we act. We study the cause, the affect and the solution for many days after a shocking crime. Prevention should be what is on the mind of law makers, parents, teachers, ministers and others who serve the general population.

Conclusion

Crime is one of the greatest threats to any society. It affects every race and sex all over this land. Crime will always be a number one priority as long as we have a continuously growing gap between the haves and have-nots. Certainly, there should not be any link between poverty and crime, but unfortunately there is.

Many people have thought their communities were safe and free from crime. But this is far from the truth because drug use has infiltrated the low-income communities as well as the high-income ones.

One of the reasons that crime is a growing threat to all communities is because people ignore or don't get involved in community actions to stop crimes. There are many other reasons why crime is increasing throughout the world and there will be very little anyone can do about it.

My experience with eradicating crime in my neighborhood has been to stay active with community watch and educate residents on the importance of keeping their property well-maintained. This will not let thieves take advantage of you because they view you as careless.

In my community, I have personally challenged the residents to take extra measures to not let crime enter our neighborhood. The majority of the residents didn't care about doing any extra work outside of their homes.

When the city failed to cut the grass entering the access way into the subdivision where I live, I decided to cut the entrance to homes myself. I personally took the time to cut the grass and maintain the entrance to show that our community cared about the way other people see it. I solicited others to help for many years, but no one else cared to help. I believe that if thieves see that you care about your community, then they might think that someone is watching to see who will mess it up.

A person will always have to take an active role in society to keep humanity safe.

I remember watching a movie about a community being invaded by criminals. They were destroying property and savagely beat a homeowner on his front lawn. The police arrived before the criminals could get away and were arrested.

Before they were carried away, the police asked if there were any witnesses to the incidents. After surveying the crowd who had witnessed the man being beaten, no one seemed to want to step forward and identify the criminals. But before the crowd and police left the scene, one lone witness reluctantly stepped forward to identify the criminals.

When the criminals bonded out of jail, they came back to harass the lone witness daily and eventually beat him. After the neighbors witnessed the courage of the victim, they stepped forward to identify the criminals.

The movie taught me at an early age that you have to stand against the wrongs committed against you even though you might suffer.

The police cannot monitor all communities and you must help to reduce crime in your community.

When we incarcerate criminals in institutions, we need to make sure they receive religious instruction along with educational opportunities. There are many prison systems that are making sure they include spiritual awareness in their prison system. Many officials say that prisoners who accept religious instruction rarely come back to prison.

Crime threatens self-preservation. America as a whole believes that any means necessary should be used to eradicate crime. This way of thinking is justified if you have ever been a victim of a violent crime. But in reality, this thinking must be marginalized because it has given rise to police brutality, forced confessions with violence and inadequate defenses for those who cannot afford to hire attorneys. The pendulum can be swung back and forth because many people believe that the victims of crime do not have enough rights. The basic premise of self-preservation comes in the form of safety and protection for all. Safety and protection can only come from service to others. Because, until the basic human needs of all people are met, there will always be a high crime rate that cannot be policed.

We desperately need stiffer gun control laws passed to keep unwanted guns off the street. Guns are the catalyst for most crimes and we need to keep them away from criminals.

Illegal drugs are tearing down the moral fabric of our society at an alarming rate. Most crimes today are committed to satisfy uncontrollable cravings for drugs. Highly addictive drugs are entering all neighborhoods and will continue to be a threat to our society. They bring all kinds of crimes to neighborhoods to support drug habits.

The most effective deterrent to crimes in neighborhoods and businesses is community watch associations. The old community way of neighbor watching neighbor is the most effective way to combat crime.

The computer age has introduced many people to crimes who never thought they would have done anything illegal. The internet is providing information to all on how to commit crimes electronically and physically.

Arming yourself with the knowledge of how criminals think is the way to survive in today's society. The more you know how a criminal thinks is the best way to not be a victim.

www.ingramcontent.com/pod-product-compliance
Lightning Source LLC
Chambersburg PA
CBHW020356270326
41926CB00007B/466